FORCED TO BE RICH

WHEN THERE IS NO OTHER ALTERNATIVE

10 INCREDIBLE RULES FOR GETTING YOU THERE

Dr. Titus C. Wright

Copyright 2019 Titus C. Wright

*This publication may not be reproduced,
stored in a retrieval system or transmitted in
whole or in part, in any form or by any means
electronic, mechanical, photocopying, recording
or otherwise, without the prior written permission
of Wright Media Group Incorporated, First Edition 2019.
Copyright 2019 Wright Media Group Inc.
For information, Contact Special Sales Department
Wright Media Group, Inc. Philadelphia PA
(Email at: twrightmediagroup@gmail.com)*

*This Publisher and Author disclaim any personal liability, loss
or risk incurred as a consequence of the use and application,
either directly or indirectly, of any advice, information or
methods presented in this publication.
Printed in the United States of America*

"Both riches and honor come of God, and he reigns over all; and in your hand is power and might: and in your hand is to make great, and to give strength unto all."

-I Chronicles 29: 12

CONTENTS

Introduction 7

A Thought 13
Chapter One 15 Ten Rules for Achieving Business Success

Rule 1 16 Start With a Realistic Strategy
Rule 2 19 Set Up your Operation
Rule 3 20 Put A System In Place
Rule 4 21 Work with Good People
Rule 5 22 Be Contribution Minded
Rule 6 23 Discipline Your Self for Success

Chapter Two 31 Creating A Wealthy Mentality
Rule 7 33 Get Out of Your Own Way
Rule 8 34 Make Yourself Rich on Purpose
Rule 9 35 Make Quality Decisions
Rule 10 35 Rediscover Your Inner Nerd

Chapter Three 39 The Conclusion
About The Author 41

NOTES

INTRODUCTION:

"Don't Look At Tomorrow With Today's Eyes. Everyday Is Different and Affords You The Opportunity To Make A Positive Change."

-Dr. T.C. Wright

Is your financial back against the wall? Are you on the verge of losing everything you worked so hard to get? Are you sick and tired of being sick and tired concerning your finance situations? If you answered yes to any one of these questions then my friend, there is a strong indication that something out there is forcing you to get rich. If you're having major problems paying your mortgage or monthly rent and you can't pay for food or your utilities, there's really one thing going on. You are being forced to be rich! When creditors are threatening to foreclose on your property, repossess your car, turn off your utilities, kick you out of school or something even worse there is only one solution, you need to be rich. You really don't need to figure out how you're going to pay any of those bills. You also don't need to worry about how you're going to meet this or that financial obligation. All of your money problems will be solved with one simple action, just be rich!

Believe it or not, it takes the same amount of energy, effort and creativity in coming up with excuses for your creditors than it takes to simply be rich. I hope you realize all of these things are happening to you for one reason. These things are forcing you to be rich. There is something out there trying to get your attention! These financial situations in your life are all saying the same thing, that you need to be rich.

How can you stop the foreclosure of your home or repossession of your car? How can you get those medical bills paid or student loan creditors from breathing down your neck? You need to be rich! Don't just think about how you can get out of debt or pay off everyone you owe. You don't need enough to just get out of debt, you need to be rich. Start thinking about how you can go beyond the break even point and get rich. You need more than just enough to get your head above water, you really need to be rich. All of your current money challenges are forcing you to get rich. That is the message being pervaded by your current financial circumstances. Listen to what it's telling you. That means you have no other alternative. You are Forced to Be Rich!

Friend this book is for you. This book represents over 25 years of business experience and training. The scriptures say that there is no new thing under the sun. These upcoming concepts have been taught for years but people are just starting to listen. After years of reading and studying hundreds of books by some of the most successful financial gurus, I realize that they all basically give much of the same advice. Success does leave clues. Their obvious overwhelming success is the proof that it works. I will be quoting lots of these people but chances are, they weren't the first to have said it.

Starting your own business isn't an exact science. It is more of an art. Successful entrepreneurs are a very diverse group of people. You should seriously consider either becoming an entrepreneur or investor. In the long run, it would be to your best financial advantage. You can have the opportunity to be self empowered and really stake your claim, as they say, *"Put your dagger in the sand"*

It is true that nobody is going to come to your rescue when you are broke, busted, and disgusted. However, I do believe there are plenty of opportunities out there that will fit into your plan, if you have one. The key word here is *plan*. You've got to have a plan or strategy to get where you want to be. Author Wallace D. Wattles mentions in his many books that getting rich is the result of *"doing things in a certain way."* You have got to associate yourself with either a product, service, or concept. If you look around you will notice that everybody is selling something. There are only two transactions taking place in the world 24 hours a day. Either you are buying or selling something. If you are employed, then you are selling your time for dollars. If you are a teacher (as in my case a professor), then you are selling your knowledge. What are your abilities, skills, or talents? What do you plan to sell or have to offer?

They often say you have to have a better idea to succeed. This is not always true. You can find something that is already doing well and do that. An I-Phone isn't the invention of the telephone. As Alexander Graham Bell already did that. The I-phone represents an incremental change from past technologies. This includes the internet, TV, camera, video, game arcade and so much more. You don't always have to reinvent the wheel. There are tons of examples of people doing what you already want to do. There are biographies you can read, people you can see or hear about that are involved in doing the same thing you desire to do right now.

As long as there is breath in your body, there is hope. You need to give yourself another opportunity because good success is what you desire. You may be wondering why I included the word *"good"* in front of the word *"success."* That's because there are two types of successes; *good and bad.* If you have never succeeded in business or in reaching your financial goals, then you have been successful at failing. However, you are not a failure unless you give up trying. Only when you give up, can we officially label you a failure. The difference between a winner and a loser is, winners never quit. I know that you are not one to give up because you are reading this book. Put it in your spirit and begin to say as Les Brown said in his 1997 best selling book titled, *"It Not Over, Until You Win!"*

My mission and vision for this book is to get you fired up about your financial future. If you have experienced failure time and time again then something needs fixing. It is possible to shake off failure and gravitate toward success. Some people only need a slight change in direction to find real and lasting success, while others may need a little more. You can become a victor instead of a victim by dropping that victim mentality. Business failure is devastating, however, you must understand that it is temporary and simply a part of the process of becoming successful. The bottom line here is to never give up and don't quit. As Donald Trump says, *"Never, ever give up! You can change and you can move around but never, ever give up!"* (Trump 1997, Art of the Comeback).

You Need to Change Your Strategy! Actor Denzel Washington said in a 2010 Dillard University graduation speech, *"To get something you've never had, you've got to do something you've never did"* Even the Bible tells us that *"You reap what you sow."*[1] What are you sowing? We first started this chapter off by saying, "Hindsight is always twenty-twenty." Become vigilant in learning from your own mistakes and bad decisions of the past. It's called paying tuition; the cost of education. You have to be awakened to it and take good notes. Have you ever said to yourself, "If I knew then, what I know now, I would have done things a whole lot differently"?

My premise in writing this book is, it has to represent what really works. It must work for me first before I can share it with others. I noticed some time ago on an office wall an inspiration poster that read, *"An ounce of action beats a ton of theory"* -Friedrich Engels.

Success is more than money, it's how you live your life

overall. Many successful people give similar advice. They say, *"Failure is inevitable, don't try to avoid it because it is going to happen."* Stallone also reminds us that, *"It's not about how hard you get hit, but how much you can take and keep moving forward. That's how winning is done." -(2007, Rocky Balbao Film).*

If you focus on a higher purpose, the money will take care of itself. You should be working with passion and true purpose. Don't do things for money, but focus on being successful and being grateful. You can apply these concepts right now when reading each chapter. Be patient, experience the difference and enjoy the process!

Seriously, how much money do you really want or need? What would it take for you to be able to finally say these words *"I'm rich, I'm rich, oops, I'm relatively comfortable"* Being rich for one person has a totally different meaning for another. Most people would be extremely happy to wake up one morning to find that their entire net-worth was around one billion dollars. They would be ecstatic, but some people wouldn't. They would seriously consider filing for bankruptcy. I'm talking about some of today's most wealthy people. Many of them have a net worth between 5 to 100 billion dollars. They would not be happy to find out their net worth went down to just $1 billion. As you can see, wealth is all relative. In other words, the cash sum amount is not the same for everyone. What is wealth to you? You need to specifically define what wealth means to you and create an achievable plan. How much money would it take for you to feel financially independent and successful? Success has to be planned and earned. The secret to this whole thing in a nutshell is, if you focus on success, wealth will always show up. If a professional boxer keeps knocking out his opponents, wealth will always follow him. This does not happen the other way around. Success is the generator of wealth. If you keep winning, you keep getting paid.

The more success, the more pay. This also happens at work too. Sometimes you have to qualify yourself for a raise by first doing more consistently, then you can ask for a raise later. If you keep this in mind you will always be prosperous. Don't get the order mixed up. No unsuccessful person has ever become wealthy. I really want you to become wealthy so badly! Whether you know it or not, people are depending on you to become rich. This is because many of them don't have the faith and motivation that you have. They see something in you and need that something to inspire them to get moving. Success is a great motivator. Success speaks louder than words.

In order to live your dreams, as Les Brown often says, you've got to first build one. If you build your dream effectively, you can then live in it.

"Build your dream so you can live your dream" -Steve Harvey *(Steve Harvey show 2017).*

You have the faith to become rich or you would not be reading this book. Open your eyes, see right in front of you. Look for those magic moments. You will affect people around you because you are about to develop and enhance your extraordinary psychology to succeed. Start seeing great opportunities otherwise disguised as problems or challenges. You've got to prepare for where you want to go.

"When you change the way you look at things, the way you look at things change" - Dr. Wayne Dyer.

Pay attention to these upcoming rules. They will help guide you toward ultimate success, wealth, and prosperity; *Wealth* plus *Success* equals *Prosperity.* We will differentiate the terminology in the ensuing chapters. Now, let's get busy!

A THOUGHT

As you read this book, I want you to realize that you need others to help you along your success journey. Don't focus on money but focus on quality service, and added value. Money will come as a result of what you bring to the market place. Ninety percent of all success comes from having a great attitude. Be willing to work smart and hard. You have to get off your butt and start moving toward your goal now! When you know where you're going and what you want, the universe has a tendency to get out of your way. The Bible say that *"A mans gift will make room for him and bring him before great men"*[2].

You need to make up your mind that being successful is a must and you have got to *do* it. Begin using words such as, *I Can, It is Possible, It's Not too Hard or Difficult for Me!* Let's be totally honest with ourselves by forgetting our ego, eliminating our pride, and being willing to get down to business *right now*. Let's try our best to focus on creating a product or service of value first and then offering it to others. Condition yourself for success. Experience a paradigm shift in habits.

It's time to get comfortable with the uncomfortable.

As they say in poker, sometimes you just need to go *"All In"*. Don't trust your brain in telling you that you are doing enough. Taking massive action includes setting aside time in

your day to focus on your success. Let me give you an extra three to four hours a day right now; *Stop Watching TV! Turn it Off!* Television makes you negative and promotes laziness. It numbs your mind and drains your motivation. Television is a good schedule killer. It's a real mind zapper. Okay! Now I just gave you at least an extra 10 or more hours a week to focus on your goal of becoming successful. There is a saying that *"Successful people have Big Libraries, Poor people have Big Television's"*.

NOTES

Chapter One

10 RULES FOR ACHIEVING BUSINESS SUCCESS

"Don't just aspire to make a living. Aspire to make a difference" -Denzel Washington

Tony and Harold were very excited to start their own magazine publication company. The business was new. They even rented office space. What a proud moment it was for them! The magazine was doing very well, so they decided to hire three employees. This was aN inspirational publication, so they prayed everyday for success. Success seemed inevitable because they had plenty of local and corporate clients that advertised in each issue. Then, one day, they changed their initial strategy and decided to charge a lot more for advertising. In other words they started to get a little greedy. They endeavored to increase their print circulation too. The cost of production would be enormous at least three times that of their last issue. They even expanded far beyond their allocated budget.

Tony and Harold lost focus on their initial business strategy. They forgot why they were in business in the first place. They lost their passion for selfless service. Their initial strategy was to provide low cost advertising to small businesses in a high quality magazine. They knew that most small businesses could not afford to advertise in main stream publications. This magazine was a good alternative for that kind of niche. They were set to capture market share from local neighborhood papers and directories. But soon money became their number one focus.

In abandoning their initial strategy, Tony and Harold decided to put up two large expensive billboards in well traveled locations. After many months had passed, they desperately needed funds to pay for those extra expenses. Their expectations were unreasonable and miscalculated. If they had not increased their production cost and stayed on track with their spending, it would have been a very successful venture. Eventually the magazine folded, a lot of debt was incurred, and their friendship ended as a result. Okay, who am I kidding? This is my story! The names have been changed to avoid throwing some of the guilty under the bus.

Sometimes, when starting out in business, it is possible to get visions of grandeur. We can be tempted to run too quickly and not cautiously in making right decisions. The thing here is to think big but start small. Let expansion happen organically when starting out in business. Never force expanding a business. Your actions have to be congruent with the vision and purpose of why you are doing what you do. What is your SOOSPC, (Strategy, Operations, Outreach, System, People, and Contribution)? The ensuing rules will explain this concept.

Rule #1: Start With A Good Realistic STRATEGY.

You need to start with a good if not great strategy. This involves your core competency or specialty that gives you the edge over others in your business. A strategy gives you your aim and plan in order to achieve your goal. A strategy answers the question?, *why am I here, what am I trying to do, and what am I all about?* Having a good strategy starts with *Why* before it considers *How!* What is your story?

You need a game plan that will direct your endeavor. It doesn't have to be the perfect plan but good enough for it to become doable as well as feasible to execute. You don't have to spend forever planning and become so overwhelmed that you never get started. I know people who are always planning and never doing. Don't get caught up in that trap. They call it paralysis of the analysis. Every business has a strategy. Your strategy is either a good one, or not so good one.

As they say, *a good plan executed today is better than a **great** plan executed tomorrow.* Even a good strategy may have to be revisited once in awhile to make sure it's still relevant and up to date. Chances are, your strategy may need tweaking along the way. Corporations such as Wal-Mart have a *Low-cost* strategy which seems simple enough. Another corporation may have a Best-Cost strategy which gives you quality merchandise for a bit more than Low-Cost. It is usually much less than the higher cost for the same quality merchandise. Why am I thinking of Target? Their strategy happens to be *Best-Cost*.

There are tons of various strategies that are used to differentiate a company from it's competitors. When you enter the game you've got to have something unique and different in order for you to stand out. What is your competitive advantage? Learn to speak the customer's language. As Jesus said to the fishermen, *"I will make you fishers of men"* [1]. Your resources are more than you think. Look around and make an assessment of your assets, strengths, core competences, specialties and particular skills. Ask yourself, "What am I pretending not to see?"

UPS has a great strategy for delivering packages. It offers a great service for prompt and efficient package delivery. The main reason why people love using UPS is because of their dependability, commitment, and dedication to getting the package delivered on time. Fed-Ex also has a unique niche, They guarantee to get your packages on time and have a great plan for contingencies too. They have an entire alternative default system in place just in case something goes wrong. Wow! The pressure is always on. These two companies have a very unique niche. You need to give people a good reason why they should buy from you. Be ready to give **higher** value than what you are paid. You can't give more in cash value but you can in usage value. What is your strategy for doing business? Why are you in business? Where do you stand out and what methods do you intend to use? Unless you can answer these questions, you're not ready to be in business. If you have true passion for what you have to offer, you can easily answer these questions.

NOTES

Rule #2: Set Up Your OPERATION (Be Effective)

Strategy is just a part of the equation. You will also need a way to operate effectively. How is this vehicle going to run? Without good operations a strategy is just a vision. Operations is the actual work that needs to be done. The UPS and FED-Ex operations are incredible. Everything is sorted using state of the art space age technology. Amazon is another company that is seemingly doing the impossible when it comes to sorting and shipping product packages. They have literally spent billions on these operating procedures. The hardware and software being used is super advanced technology. Their robotics are extremely efficient, time and money saving, as well as amazingly entertaining to watch.

Having thorough operations in your small business allows you to start putting things in place which is very important. Don't wait for your company to grows to then start being professional. Start now while you are small. Make your service or product a high standard commodity. Have an attitude of professionalism when interacting with customers. Be a person of high integrity and great ethics. Do what you said you would do, even to your own inconvenience. Show customers that they can trust you and your word. Develop a policy of excellence. If you do all of these things, money will never be an issue.

Who is going to do *what* in your business? It is similar to a movie producer bringing everyone together and putting them in their proper places according to their roles. At the initial start, you may be wearing most of the hats but at least you will know what these hats are. Get the most essential things you really need for the business to operate effectively. It should be a service business to start, thus less overhead. Operations is simply the physical follow through of actions in your strategy (vision). It's the *how* to your *why*. Remember, a company is just a group of people. What is your *outreach*? Exactly who are you trying to reach? You are a company of one right now. It's up to you to: *Just Do It!*

Rule #3: Put A SYSTEM In Place. (Be Efficient)

Now that you have gathered all of the necessary tools needed for your business to operate, you need to put them in proper order and working efficiently. You have to be able to measure progress as well. If you are not measuring progress, you will not know if your efficiency is working effectively. Are these things actually working in the most efficient way? Make sure no efforts are being wasted. Is it automated to avoid redundancy? This also includes you as a business owner in how you run your time. Anything you usually do three or four times a day, try and do it once a day. This means when checking emails, phone calls, meetings etc. Have a specific time allocated for each activity, once a day only. Try your best to avoid unnecessary distractions. Measure, measure and measure your progress. As they say, *"You only can expect what you inspect."*

UPS's system for routing the drivers to better efficiency is ingenious as well as money saving. Just having drivers avoiding left turns saves the company millions of dollars a year. You also need to have a system for changing what doesn't work.

A good system represents structure for operating your business. Your operation should be automated into a good working system. When you put a system in place. you are actually putting order and efficiency in your business. Why are so many highly educated people with all kinds of degrees not rich? They have tons of knowledge, but no image to follow in putting it all together. It's like having all the one thousand pieces to a puzzle and no image on the box to see what to put together. We need direction. We need systems. This is how you get things to run as they say, like a "well oiled machine."

Rule #4: Work With Good PEOPLE.

Warren Buffet often says, you should try and hire people with integrity, intelligence and energy. He does caution that if the first attribute is not there (integrity), then you want them dumb and lazy. In his books Donald Trump admits that he has issues with just good or average employees. He wants them to be great employees. Trump says a bad employee can easily be fired. A great employee will be one you want to keep because they are phenomenal. However, a good or average employee is the worst employee because they do just enough to keep their job. Trump believes that they never take you to the next level but you can't really fire them. He mentions how frustrating they are to him.

Speaking of employees, you can begin with volunteers or students (interns) on a part time basis. This would be wise since cash is scarce when first starting your business. If you make people feel part of the business, they will want to help you to succeed. Don't take your business personally. See it for what it is, a business. Do things for the good of the business, not for the good of yourself. See yourself as an employee of your venture. Set rules and abide by them. Become a team player with customers and others in business. There is nothing better for your business than for a customer to let you know what they really want.

Try to develop as many business relationships with other entrepreneurs as possible, even if you don't have much interest in their business. Be open to changes, quick maneuvers, and adjustments. Never be stone faced. Always be willing to make practical changes to accommodate your customers. Never take the *"It's my way or the highway"* attitude, or you will be on a lonely highway broke. I'm not saying change with the wind.

However, change only if it absolutely makes sense. Constantly seek criticism from anyone you can, especially from your friends. You can also take advantage of on-line communities all over the world from people who may be able to help you. Listen to everybody from the bust boy to corporate CEO's. However, only work with people with good ethics.

If you believe that you have a great business idea or service that people really need, then all you have to do is get them to know about it and want it. Haven't you noticed that people do not always buy what they need. They buy what they want. Children do not take their extra money and buy vegetables and nutritious foods. They usually buy what they want, like junk food. Simply ask yourself this question: "If I were a customer, would I be excited about what I am selling?" If you're not, as they say, *head over heels,* then no one else will be either. It's not really work if you enjoy what you do. I wish you much success with this one.

Rule #5: Be CONTRIBUTION Minded (Give).

Contribution would complete your realistic plan. What are you willing to give for your success? It is a true statement, "*You have to give something to get something.*" Think about your contribution to the community, customers, workers or etc. Be willing to *give* something first. If making money is your only goal for being in business, then success will be delayed. I'm not saying start a charity. What I am asking is, what do you intend to give for your success? They call it your *social responsibility.*

The way out of your financial dilemma is to give. You need to start giving and avoid simply trading. Trading is giving equal value for equal value. As they say, *tit for tat.* This is not truly giving. Giving goes beyond measuring equal value, but extends beyond what has been received. Many successful corporations tithe a portion of their profit. The way out of a deficit is in your giving. Your financial deliverance is an inside job. Give people a reason to buy from you. Think of it as, *What's In It For You (WIIFY)* attitude. *The You* represents the other person. What can you give to others first? Giving is a good way to network with others. It helps you build relationships faster. If you go to a business seminar or networking event, look to serve. Collect cards and ask what it would take to bring them business. Be interested in others first and ask them questions about their business. You will be the most interesting person in the room because everybody else is doing the opposite. In order to be interesting, you've got to be interested in other people's concerns. Your giving should be in areas where you have some strengths. Learn to give and grow rich. Financial success buys you your freedom. Learn to add to others and not subtract. As mentioned before, be a *go- giver* and not a *taker*. Consider tithing. Tithing is at least ten

percent of your income. It gives the universe an invested interest in what you are doing. The good feeling you get when giving creates a wealth mentality and great ideas are created within that premise. Instead of asking God to give you more money, ask for great ideas. He will give if you will give. You don't want to be at an impasse with God. The old folks used to say, *"You can't beat God giving, no matter how hard you try"*. Giving represents the seed sown by you. I always receive much more than what I had sown. Any farmer will confirm that fact. Once, I gave a very large offering to a church and three weeks later, my lawyer called me. He wanted me to pick up a very large unexpected second check from a past settlement. Giving unbelievably works! Don't neglect your *overall contribution.*

Rule #6: DISCIPLINE Yourself For Success..

The first employee of your business is *You*. Are you disciplined for growth? Discipline creates freedom. Discipline yourself for success by creating and forming wealth habits. You have to have an emotional investment in what you are doing. You need discipline in handling money. Try to increase your financial acumen by reading. Having tons of money with no discipline is like driving a car at one hundred miles an hour with no steering wheel and no brakes. You're eventually going to end up in a crash. If you take a speeding locomotive off the track, where does it go? Success demands discipline. Ideas create wealth which generates money/cash flow. Also, remember to have good values and never lie about anything. Be disciplined to tell the truth and you will prosper.

I used to rehearse being wealthy until I got good at it. This is the only way it can actually become a reality. You've got to have a burning desire with your dream. Healthy and wealthy situations are created from healthy and wealthy thoughts. If a good idea is going to come into your head, it will only come when your mind is open for it. Good feelings create good thoughts. Discipline your mind to think uplifting thoughts. As we mentioned earlier, if you want to be a winner, you have to *think* like a winner. The scriptures tell us, *"...whatsoever things are true, honest, just, pure, lovely, of good report, if there be any virtue, and praise, think on these things."*

Being down and defeated creates more down and defeated situations. No one really fails. They just get results. Sometimes those results may not always be what we expected. Learn from those unfavorable results and make the proper changes as a result. Don't look at bad results as failure or it will attract *more* failure. Remember, *like attracts like*. What are you attracting? I'm not saying pretend that everything is great. I'm saying just don't dwell on those negative thoughts because it won't help you in becoming successful. Good ideas thrive on fertile ground. You can have the best seeds, but where they're planted is crucial. If you plant them in gravel or sand, nothing will grow. Good seeds need good soil. Good ideas are generated/revealed in the good soil of your mind.

One favorite scripture of mine is, *"....but be ye transformed by the renewing of your mind..."*[3] Stay in a positive mental state. It is crucial toward your success. Be very careful about what and how you are thinking. *Proverbs states, "The thoughts of the diligent tend only to plenteousness, but everyone that is hasty only to want."*[4]

In order to make the right decisions, you must stay connected and eliminate all negative thoughts. Many wealthy people have disciplined themselves so well that certain habits are instilled in them. I call it *Unconscious Competence.* Some of them do not purchase brand new automobiles. They get to save thousands on quality leftover vehicles only a few years older. As an entrepreneur, try as much as possible to save anywhere you can. You don't always have to buy things brand new.

Purchase quality used furniture, equipment and any other necessities needed for business. You really should start your business at home first, then branch out when necessary. I've had some of my best successes in my home. I had very low overhead. I was able to really save lots of money by starting my business at home.

Are you aware that small business growth is being fueled by women, minorities, immigrants and young people who are looking for alternatives to traditional employment? Welcome to the 21st century! They know that job security is a thing of the past. Today, people aren't looking to stay at a job for 20 to 30 years. They know, in many cases this no longer exists. Even the government knows that. This is why you only have to stay at a job between 5 to 7 years to be vested and eligible to claim a pension from that job when you turn 55 years old. Again, you should consider starting a service business. This also helps alleviate many expenses by not having to produce a product.

Stop trying to figure out how to spend more money until you start making some. Develop the habits of a disciplined successful person. Invest your time first and not your money. Half the things you think you need, you don't really need. Humble yourself and get busy making money. I know what you might be saying, "How am I going to look successful and impressive if my office doesn't look impressive?" The answer to this is to always carry yourself in a professional and successful manner. I read a book years ago entitled *People Buy You* by Jeb Blount. He gives the real secret to what matters most in business. Even if you were about to buy a stock, you should always look at the CEO's mission and vision for the company. Check out who this person really is.

Most people are looking at you, the business owner, not your office. They want to first see the kind of person that you are before investing or buying from you. Are you a person of integrity, honesty and intelligence? In most cases it's a matter of trust, especially when it comes to selecting a contractor or home improvement company. If you had a good month in revenues, instead of celebrating by spending money, it would be more prudent to pay some bills in advance. This will keep you on top of things just in case you have a slump in business. If you make it important it becomes important. Discipline your mind not to worry so much. Become conscious of your thoughts, think positive thoughts. Don't let fear grip you! In his book Miracle Power for Infinite Riches, author Joseph Campbell says *"The cave we fear to enter, holds the treasure we seek"*. Try to focus on having a good outcome.

You have to see it in your mind and discipline yourself to laugh and smile at your bills. Create a good feeling for yourself because feelings create the blessing. As I mentioned before, no good ideas can come out of a worried mind. Two things cannot occupy the same space at the same time. Occupy your mind with hope, and faith that things are going to be okay. Create a positive self image for yourself and visualize it. All turn a-round's are usually changes in belief. When you have limiting beliefs, you have limitations.

"Most people, when their heart stops beating, it's just a formality because they never really lived" -(Bob Proctor- The Secret).

CONT...RULE NUMBER 6

The number one business killer is *worry*. You won't have to worry about bills if you plan ahead. Your main focus won't be divided between the next idea and how you are going to pay your bills. Financial deficits create a *"victim"* mentality.
You have to move on a solution. This causes you to look ahead and become proactive toward future financial concerns.
"Fear is living in the past, worry is living in the future and happiness is living in the now"- (Cheryl Gilman -Doing work you love)

There is nothing better than peace of mind. I'm not saying to tie all your money up with extreme preplanning. I am saying to plan for the future and be wise. You need to begin to take charge over your outcomes. It all starts with discipline toward your money. Give yourself a chance to breath and not be strangled by bills. Your skill and talent is enough to get your there but discipline keeps you there. Discipline is a major facture to your success.

NOTES

"Do what you can as well as you can do it, even if it is something you don't like"
-Bob Proctor

"Simplicity is the highest form of sophistication"
-Leonardo Da Vinci

"Some say, if I had more money I would have a better plan, but it should be, If I had a better plan, I would have more money"
-Brian Tracy

"If your ship doesn't come in, Swim out to meet it"
-Les Brown

"How you do anything, is how you do everything"
-Jack Canfield

"Massive action creates massive results"
-Grant Cardone

"Imagination and knowledge is the key to becoming successful"
-Donald J. Trump

NOTES

Chapter Four
Rules 7-10 CONT.
ACHIEVING BUSINESS SUCCESS; CREATE A WEALTHY MENTALITY

"When you solve your problems you create money, When you solve other peoples problems you create wealth."

-Dr. Eric Thomas

There are two types of people in the world, the *stoic* and the *epicurean*. I tend to lean toward the *stoic*. The *stoic* person is willing to sacrifice now for later benefits. This person knows how to exercise discipline and restraint. This is called delayed gratification. *Stoic* people remain focused on the journey of success and prosperity.

The *Epicurean* person lives for the now. They are extravagant and are constant consumers of things for pleasure and self gratification. They have the *"you only live once"* attitude. This may be true but they try and live it **all at once**. The words discipline, restraint and sacrifice are repulsive to them. Therefore most middle class epicureans are in debt and have bad credit. Poverty hovers over the epicureans on a consistent basis. When they receive any kind of funds, they spend it as soon as possible. Ted Johnson was a regular UPS worker for decades. Ted was a very stoic person. When he died at age 90, his net-worth was over 70 million dollars although his annual income was barely over $14,000 dollars. Okay, in all honesty $14,000 in 1952 is about $124,000 in today's dollars. However, he learned how to save and invest his money. He was able to give away $36 million to charity. He learned how to win against poverty and became rich as a result. Everybody should be able to save something from each pay check.

Let's face it, in most cases, being poor is the result of having had lost a fight with poverty. On the other hand, being rich is the result of winning a fight against poverty. Riches are their own reward for the victory. This fight with poverty is the fight of your life and for your very existence. You really need to win this one. Declare war against poverty today! This is not a passive war and you've got to be the aggressor. You have to win this fight to survive. Poverty is always ready to fight 24/7, even when you are asleep. Many wealthy people continue to win this war by making money while they're asleep. Companies such as Amazon and Ebay are making money every minute of the hour, seven days a week. They know that poverty never takes a break. You don't want to be caught off guard. Don't underestimate the persistence of poverty. Begin to gain a new perspective about poverty because it is always looking for your weak spots. You need to get rid of pride and arrogance because poverty thrives on these things. Sometimes poverty can be too strong to fight alone. You may need to get some help to fight in this main event.

You've got to fight poverty like it is a real person. Be ready to use defensive and offensive tactics against it. Poverty creates victims, but wealth creates victors. Develop an arsenal of defense against poverty. Put up a good fight of faith because if you hang in there, you will win this fight for you and your family. Even though poverty may put up a good fight, you should begin to prepare yourself for this battle. You've got to have the right kind of ammunition by strengthening your intellectual muscles. This is done by immersing yourself in reading and studying the biographies of successful people and their work habits. Learn their wealth principles, philosophies, strategies and their concepts. You need to give it all you've got, all of the time, with everything that is in you to win this war. Put it in your mind to destroy poverty forever. *"You don't pay the price for success, you enjoy the price of success" -(Zig Ziglar, 1977, See You at the Top).* Let's begin to explore some key rules in defeating poverty. If you want to be a winner, you must study winners. The next piece information I'm about to share with you need your full attention. True wealth is generated on the *inside* of you.

If you change your words, you'll change your world. Stop begging for opportunities and create your own. Watch what you say when you talk to yourself and others. Don't try and talk yourself out of a good idea. Focus on what you can do *now*. Give yourself the gift of time. Command your actions verbally. Go after opportunities don't wait for them to come to you. Stop looking for easy things or trying to get something for nothing.

"Don't search for opportunity in the distance but recognize them right where you are" -(Napoleon Hill, Think & Grow Rich).

Make yourself responsible for your money. Study how rich people think. You don't need more money. You need more *ideas*. You need a real money making machine idea or a cash-cow concept. You need the power to get wealthy, not a bunch of get rich gimmicks thrown at you. Remember what I said earlier. Undisciplined money won't solve your money problems, Your mind solves money problems. You need to learn how to master your thinking so you can master your money and generate cash flow. Develop your mind in areas of handling money wisely. Create something important that the world really needs instead of thinking about how to get big really fast. Your world represents the people around you. Be a person of purpose and drive.

Rule #7: *Get Out Of Your Own Way!*

Wealthy people do things a whole lot differently from poor people. Listen to what people are saying about your business. If you hear the same things two or three times, take note. Let your customers or even potential customers help you to help them. Listen to what they are saying about your product or service. Some film actors and directors enjoy going to the theater along with moviegoers, just to hear the audience's true reaction to their films. In order to stay in business, you must hear the truth. This will help you to make adjustments in how to best serve your customers. If you hear people with the same complaints about your business, then use the feedback to correct things. If you hear the same compliments, then do more of that. You should make it your habit to constantly seek criticism. Don't be afraid of the truth. You Can Handle It!

Rule #8: *Make Yourself Rich on Purpose!*

Becoming rich is an art. Don't study poverty. Abraham Lincoln said, *"You can't help the poor by being one of them."* Focus on the cure not the problem. You cannot be friends with poverty if you want to be rich. Poverty has to be your enemy. You can't love both riches and poverty. You need to hate one and cleave to the other. Remember, they are direct opposites.

If you want to help the poor, become rich. Let's face it, *"You can't help nobody if you ain't got no money!"* Do yourself and others a favor; *Become Rich!* You have got to do this for yourself and your family. Begin to operate in an abundant mentality. You can actually pay you bills with a good idea. (I have)! See poverty as a myth. The only real thing is wealth.

"Do things in life the way other people don't do them. Change the status quo, then you'll succeed." -Sheldon Adelson, (Youtube interview 2009)

TV's Shark Tank co-host Mark Cuban says that, *"You should begin to visualize your product or service as every customer or business using it."*

You need to be honest with yourself and ask, "What would wealth give you that you don't already have?" If it is just a feeling, then you need to start feeling wealthy now! All of the money in the world is spent on feeling good. Not having money is a disgrace and an embarrassment. Being without and in need is down right humiliating. Put it in your head that being prosperous is in God's plan for you. It's all up to you to feel successful. You need to begin to feel like a winner before you can actually become one. Years ago when I didn't have a penny to my name, no one knew it by looking at me. I carried myself with a wealth mentality. Only your disposition and attitude can give your situation away. I've always walked like a winner. This is how I started becoming successful. Being poor isn't cool, so get with the program. There are approximately 11 million millionaires in this country and according to Forbes magazine, there are 1,542 billionaires in the world. Most of them are entrepreneurs. This proves that there is no shortage of wealth. Abundance is everywhere!

The Bible states, *"It is better to give than to receive."*[1] That means if you are in a position to give then you are blessed but you must *have* something to give. It also says in Ephesians,
"... but rather let him labor, working with his hands the thing which is good, that he may have to give to him that is in need"
Bob Proctor believes, *"You Were Born Rich" -(The Secret movie, 2007)*

You must study the wealthy and start giving to others. Conduct business as honestly and as professionally as possible and position yourself for success. Why *you should* be rich? Because it is a must for you. It's up to you to save your own little world and come to your own rescue. Author Grant Cardone states, *"Being Rich is your Duty, Obligation and Responsibility".* That's why you're getting *Forced To Be Rich!*

Rule #9: *Make Quality Decisions.*

In business, there will always be difficult decisions to make. However, there will also be difficult decisions that really don't have to be made right away. Don't be afraid to sleep on a decision. You'll be surprised what the next day will bring. Some of these decisions might include whether to expand, offer a new product or service, advertise, purchase, rent, hire or fire someone, etc. Some people may expand too early and realize they really should have waited. If what you are about to do in your business has a chance of failing and you know you will not be able to recover financially, then don't do it until you are sure. I like calculated risks better than gambling. A calculated risk prepares for contingencies. Gambling does not. Be wise in business and be careful when making decisions. Never put yourself in a *go for broke* situation. As they say, don't put all of your eggs in one basket, If you do, then watch that basket like a hawk.

Don't be in a rush. You need to absolutely feel comfortable with the pros and cons of either result. Make a list of the advantages and disadvantages, then compare both lists. Get the pros and cons of each on paper in front of you. Then you will be able to see the possibilities and make an intelligent decision. This always works for me. If you have a business idea that is not working and it's causing you to lose money, then re-evaluate it. Don't just sit there and die letting precious weeks, months, even years pass by while waiting for a miracle. Be prepared to do what is necessary. After a few weeks of lost revenues, it is time for you to realize that something needs changing. You can prayerfully do one of two things: Either scrap the business completely and stop the bleeding or change your business strategy. Consider one of those options, if you doubt that your service or product is not really what people are looking for or need. Consider another business idea. However, if you know in your heart of hearts and feel in your gut that your business is very much needed, then stay the course. At this point, consider changing your strategy.

You must be people oriented in order to survive and make your business work. Much success!

Rule #10: *Rediscover Your Inner Nerd!*

Read or listen to something about business everyday, be It business books, magazines, biographies, Youtube videos, etc. You Must Continue to Stimulate Your Mind! You've got to stay informed on what is going on now. When you do become successful, eradicate the feeling that you have "made it", this is a dangerous position. Multi-billionaire investor Warren Buffet tells people to have a sense of restlessness and to act as if someone is always after you. To tell you the truth, they are. Someone is always in line to try and take food out of your mouth. Get on a mission and put everything you have into the study of wealthy and successful people. Ask tons of questions. You will find that people love talking about themselves and are eager for someone to listen to them. Be dogmatic about your mission. Don't think you are bothering them when asking questions because you are not. Even if you are, so what! This is not a nice game. This is a game of life or death!

Yes, be polite as possible but stay on course with your mission. Become a brain picker. Don't hesitate to compliment others in admiring their success by telling them. Tell successful people that you respect and honor them. They will want to help you to succeed too. If you are a younger person, most successful older people want to reminisce of when they got started. They may even see themselves in you when they were your age. You'll be surprised at how open they will be with you.

You should never, ever be a hater of other people's success as it will work against you. You will be programming your subconscious mind to hate wealthy and successful people. Your subconscious mind will make sure it doesn't happen to you. It will protect you from what you hate, thinking it is doing you a favor. This is why you should be happy when you hear of other people's good fortunes. If someone you know gets a raise or a new job, a new automobile or anything good, just be happy for them. Your subconscious mind will try and make these things happen for you too. You will be guided toward successful ideas.

You need to stay up to date and informed concerning new technologies and what's coming next. I heard it said that readers are leaders. I read and study tons of information and am able to recall most of it, thanks to memory techniques. I try to read at least one book a week. One of the biggest habits of the extremely wealthy is that they read a lot. Rich people are quick to hear and slow to speak. That's why they "know stuff". Close your mouth and open your ears. Let your learning lead to wealth. Brian Tracy believes that, *"You should work harder on yourself than you do on your job."* Study successful people by reading about them. Let the library or bookstore be your friend!

Reading is an essential ingredient to having a successful business. You will find that the more you read, the more you want to read. Reading about other successful people and the challenges they overcame to succeed will help to motivate you. Reading gives you a fresh perspective on things and more to share with others. Leaders inspire action. Reading increases your knowledge like nothing else. Remember that old but true saying, *Reading is Fundamental*!

NOTES

Chapter Three

CONCLUSION OF THE WHOLE MATTER:

"Those that can see the invisible can do the impossible".
- Tyrese

Congratulations! By now, you should be seeing changes in your life. Some people believe that the amount of money a person makes is important. I believe what you do with whatever money you have is more important. However, doing what you really love while meeting a need and serving others is the *Key* to fulfillment. This is extremely important! These practical concepts are just the beginning.

This book's subtitle does mention *Wealth, Success,* and *Prosperity*. These three appear to be the same, however, they are not. Wealth is moving forward with no particular state of emotion. It could be summed up as cash flow. Success is an internal feeling or state of being. It is a state of mind derived from fulfillment. Prosperity is the combination of them both being in balance and congruent with each other. It is possible to be wealthy without feeling successful. Success gives wealth meaning. Inherited wealth needs meaning attached to it. This is why so many wealthy people become philanthropists, give to charities or start foundations. Now that you have completed this reading, use the information in this book as a reference. Refer to it often. When you can't see your way clear financially just be reminded that the *Force Is With You*! Something is driving you to make a change in your life. You may actually are being Forced To Be Rich! Keep this book close to you for continued guidance toward making wise decisions for Achievement, Success, Wealth and Prosperity in your life.

Congratulations!

ABOUT THE AUTHOR

Dr. Titus C. Wright is a motivational speaker, expert sales trainer, university professor, and CEO of Wright Media Group. He is the inspired author of *How To Get The Man/Woman of Your Dreams, Waiting To Be Great* and *Why You Should Be Rich.*

Titus motivates thousands of people per week with his *Positive Force* Youtube videos. magazine publications, and self help books. He is blessed to have earned two Masters degrees in business administration/management. He also received a (Ph.D.) in Christian Education. Titus has dedicated his life to personal self development and in helping others find their true purpose and passion. He has appeared on local and national television shows, numerous radio programs and in newsprint/magazines. He lives in Pennsylvania with his lovely wife, Coral.

FORCE TO BE RICH is Titus's fifth nationwide book release. This book is considered by far, one of the most revealing, straight forward and helpful to date. It is said by many that his books are worth their weight in *Pure Gold*. His multi-media organization continues to thrive due to these God-given rules. He adheres to his own advice and has been able to implement these concepts in his own life and business. Titus believes that, prosperity isn't about owning things. It's about nothing owning you! Contact email: twrightmediagroup@gmail.com

Available for corporate and academic speaking engagements.

Other Books By Dr. Titus C. Wright

How To Get The Woman Of Your Dreams & Man of Your Dreams

Two, One of a Kind Books That Every Person Should Have In Their Personal Collection

GO TO AMAZON.COM/DR. TITUS C. WRIGHT

www.ingramcontent.com/pod-product-compliance
Lightning Source LLC
Chambersburg PA
CBHW071152220526
45468CB00003B/1031